JB

by John Berryman

JOHN BERRYMAN

Short Poems

FARRAR, STRAUS & GIROUX

NEW YORK

Contents

THE DISPOSSESSED

TO MY MOTHER

I

Winter Landscape

The three men coming down the winter hill
In brown, with tall poles and a pack of hounds
At heel, through the arrangement of the trees,
Past the five figures at the burning straw,
Returning cold and silent to their town,

Returning to the drifted snow, the rink
Lively with children, to the older men,
The long companions they can never reach,
The blue light, men with ladders, by the church
The sledge and shadow in the twilit street,

Are not aware that in the sandy time
To come, the evil waste of history
Outstretched, they will be seen upon the brow
Of that same hill: when all their company
Will have been irrecoverably lost,

These men, this particular three in brown
Witnessed by birds will keep the scene and say
By their configuration with the trees,
The small bridge, the red houses and the fire,
What place, what time, what morning occasion

Sent them into the wood, a pack of hounds
At heel and the tall poles upon their shoulders,
Thence to return as now we see them and
Ankle-deep in snow down the winter hill
Descend, while three birds watch and the fourth flies.

The Statue

The statue, tolerant through years of weather,
Spares the untidy Sunday throng its look,
Spares shopgirls knowledge of the fatal pallor
Under their evening colour,
Spares homosexuals, the crippled, the alone,
Extravagant perception of their failure;
Looks only, cynical, across them all
To the delightful Avenue and its lights.

Where I sit, near the entrance to the Park,
The charming dangerous entrance to their need,
Dozens, a hundred men have lain till morning
And the preservative darkness waning,
Waking to want, to the day before, desire
For the ultimate good, Respect, to hunger waking;
Like the statue ruined but without its eyes;
Turned vaguely out at dawn for a new day.

Fountains I hear behind me on the left,
See green, see natural life springing in May
To spend its summer sheltering our lovers,
Those walks so shortly to be over.
The sound of water cannot startle them
Although their happiness runs out like water,
Of too much sweetness the expected drain.
They trust their Spring; they have not seen the statue.

Disfigurement is general. Nevertheless
Winters have not been able to alter its pride,
If that expression is a pride remaining,
Coriolanus and Rome burning,

An aristocracy that moves no more.
Scholars can stay their pity; from the ceiling
Watch blasted and superb inhabitants,
The wreck and justifying ruined stare.

Since graduating from its years of flesh
The name has faded in the public mind
Or doubled: which is this? the elder? younger?
The statesman or the traveller?
Who first died or who edited his works,
The lonely brother bound to remain longer
By a quarter-century than the first-born
Of that illustrious and lost family?

The lovers pass. Not one of them can know
Or care which Humboldt is immortalized.
If they glance up, they glance in passing,
An idle outcome of that pacing
That never stops, and proves them animal;
These thighs breasts pointed eyes are not their choosing,
But blind insignia by which are known
Season, excitement, loosed upon this city.

Turning: the brilliant Avenue, red, green,
The laws of passage; marvellous hotels;
Beyond, the dark apartment where one summer
Night an insignificant dreamer,
Defeated occupant, will close his eyes
Mercifully on the expensive drama
Wherein he wasted so much skill, such faith,
And salvaged less than the intolerable statue.

The Disciple

Summoned from offices and homes, we came.
By candle-light we heard him sing;
We saw him with a delicate length of string
Hide coins and bring a paper through a flame;
I was amazed by what that man could do.
And later on, in broad daylight,
He made someone sit suddenly upright
Who had lain long dead and whose face was blue.

But most he would astonish us with talk.
The warm sad cadence of his voice,
His compassion, and our terror of his choice,
Brought each of us both glad and mad to walk
Beside him in the hills after sundown.
He spoke of birds, of children, long
And rubbing tribulation without song
For the indigent and crippled of this town.

Ventriloquist and strolling mage, from us,
Respectable citizens, he took
The hearts and swashed them in an upland brook,
Calling them his, all men's, anonymous.
. . He gained a certain notoriety;
The magical outcome of such love
The State saw it could not at all approve
And sought to learn where when that man would be.

The people he had entertained stood by,
I was among them, but one whom
He harboured kissed him for the coppers' doom,
Repenting later most most bitterly.

They ran him down and drove him up the hill.
He who had lifted but hearts stood
With thieves, performing still what tricks he could
For men to come, rapt in compassion still.

Great nonsense has been spoken of that time.
But I can tell you I saw then
A terrible darkness on the face of men,
His last astonishment; and now that I'm
Old I behold it as a young man yet.
None of us now knows what it means,
But to this day our loves and disciplines
Worry themselves there. We do not forget.

A Point of Age

I

At twenty-five a man is on his way.
The desolate childhood smokes on the dead hill,
My adolescent brothels are shut down
For industry has moved out of that town;
Only the time-dishonoured beggars and
The flat policemen, victims, I see still.
Twenty-five is a time to move away.

The travelling hands upon the tower call,
The clock-face telescopes a long desire:
Out of the city as the autos stream
I watch, I whisper, Is it time . . time?
Fog is enveloping the bridges, lodgers
Shoulder and fist each other in the mire
Where later, leaves, untidy lives will fall.

Companions, travellers, by luck, by fault
Whose none can ever decide, friends I had
Have frozen back or slipt ahead or let
Landscape juggle their destinations, slut
Solace and drink drown the degraded eye.
The fog is settling and the night falls, sad,
Across the forward shadows where friends halt.

Images are the mind's life, and they change.
How to arrange it—what can one afford
When ghosts and goods tether the twitching will
Where it has stood content and would stand still
If time's map bore the brat of time intact?
Odysseys I examine, bed on a board,
Heartbreak familiar as the heart is strange.

In the city of the stranger I discovered
Strike and corruption: cars reared on the bench
To horn their justice at the citizen's head
And hallow the citizen deaf, half-dead.
The quiet man from his own window saw
Insane wind take the ash, his favourite branch
Wrench, crack; the hawk came down, the raven hovered.

Slow spent stars wheel and dwindle where I fell.
Physicians are a constellation where
The blown brain sits a fascist to the heart.
Late, it is late, and it is time to start.
Sanction the civic woe, deal with your dear,
Convince the stranger: none of us is well.
We must travel in the direction of our fear.

II

By what weird ways, Mather and Boone, we came.
Ethan Allen, father, in the rebel wood
Teach trust and disobedience to the son
Who neither obeys nor can disobey One
No longer, down the reaches of his longing, known.
Speak from the forest and declare my blood
Dishonour, a trick a mockery my name.

You, Shaver, other shade, rébel again,
Great-grandfather, attest my hopeless need
Amongst the chromium luxury of the age
Uncomfortable, threadbare, apt to rage.
Recall your office, exile; tell me now
To devour the annals of the valuable dead,
Fish for the cortex, candour for my pain.

Horizons perish from a hacking eye! . .
The Hero, haggard on the top of time,
Enacts his inconceivable woe and pride
Plunging his enemies down the mountainside,
Lesson and master. We are come to learn
Compassion from the last and piercing scream
Of who was lifted before he could die.

Animal-and-Hero, where you lounge the air
Is the air of summer, smooth and masculine
As skin over a muscle; but the day
Darkens, and it is time to move away.
Old friends unbolt the night wherein you roam;
Wind rises, lightning, rain beats, you begin
The climb the conflict that are your desire.

In storm and gloom, before it is too late
I make my testament. I bequeath my heart
To the disillusioned few who have wished me well;
My vision I leave to one who has the will
To master it, and the consuming art;
What else—the sorrow, the disease, the hate—
I scatter; and I am prepared to start.

III
What is the age of naked man? His time
Scrawls the engrossing tumult on green mould
In a cellar and disreputable place.
Consternation and Hope war in his face.
Writhing upon his bed who achieves sleep
Who is alone? Man in the cradle, old,
Rocks on the fiery earth, smoke is his fame.

Prophecy is another smoke, and lost.
To say that country, time to come, will be
The island or harbour city of our choice
Argues the sick will raving in the voice.
The pythoness is mute upon her bier,
Cassandra took a thrust she would not see
And dropt for daughter an inarticulate ghost.

The animal within the animal
How shall we satisfy? With toys its fear,
With incantation its adorable trust?
Shall we say 'We were once and we shall be dust'
Or nourish it with confident lies and look
Contentment? What can the animal bear?
Whose version brightens that will not appal?

Watch in the valleys for the sign of snow.
Watch the light. Where the riotous leaves lay
Will arise a winter man at the New Year
And speak. No eye will be dry, none shall fear.
—That time is not yet, and our eyes are now:
Twenty-five is a time to move away.
Late on the perilous wood the son flies low.

The projection of the tower on the pine
Wavers. The wind will fan and force the fire
Streaming across our ditches to find wood.
All that someone has wished or understood
Is fuel to the holocaust he lives;
It spreads, it is the famine of his desire,
The tongue teeth eyes of your will and of mine.

What then to praise, what love, what look to have?
The animals who lightless live, alone
And dark die. We await the rising moon.
When the moon lifts, lagging winter moon,
Its white face over time where the sun shone
Gold once, we have a work to do, a grave
At last for the honourable and exhausted man.

DETROIT, *1940*

The Traveller

They pointed me out on the highway, and they said
'That man has a curious way of holding his head.'

They pointed me out on the beach; they said 'That man
Will never become as we are, try as he can.'

They pointed me out at the station, and the guard
Looked at me twice, thrice, thoughtfully & hard.

I took the same train that the others took,
To the same place. Were it not for that look
And those words, we were all of us the same.
I studied merely maps. I tried to name
The effects of motion on the travellers,
I watched the couple I could see, the curse
And blessings of that couple, their destination,
The deception practised on them at the station,
Their courage. When the train stopped and they knew
The end of their journey, I descended too.

The Ball Poem

What is the boy now, who has lost his ball,
What, what is he to do? I saw it go
Merrily bouncing, down the street, and then
Merrily over—there it is in the water!
No use to say 'O there are other balls':
An ultimate shaking grief fixes the boy
As he stands rigid, trembling, staring down
All his young days into the harbour where
His ball went. I would not intrude on him,
A dime, another ball, is worthless. Now
He senses first responsibility
In a world of possessions. People will take balls,
Balls will be lost always, little boy.
And no one buys a ball back. Money is external.
He is learning, well behind his desperate eyes,
The epistemology of loss, how to stand up
Knowing what every man must one day know
And most know many days, how to stand up
And gradually light returns to the street,
A whistle blows, the ball is out of sight,
Soon part of me will explore the deep and dark
Floor of the harbour . . I am everywhere,
I suffer and move, my mind and my heart move
With all that move me, under the water
Or whistling, I am not a little boy.

Fare Well

Motions of waking trouble winter air,
I wonder, and his face as it were forms
Solemn, canorous, under the howled alarms,—
The eyes shadowed and shut.
Certainly for this sort of thing it is very late,
I shudder, while my love longs and I pour
My bright eyes towards the moving shadow . . where?
Out, like a plucked gut.

What has been taken away will not return,
I take it, whether upon the crouch of night
Or for my mountain need to share a morning's light,—
No! I am alone.
What has been taken away should not have been shown,
I complain, torturing, and then withdrawn.
After so long, can I still long so and burn,
Imperishable son?

O easy the phoenix in the tree of the heart,
Each in its time, his twigs and spices fixes
To make a last nest, and marvellously relaxes,—
Out of the fire, weak peep! . .
Father I fought for Mother, sleep where you sleep!
I slip into a snowbed with no hurt
Where warm will warm be warm enough to part
Us. As I sink, I weep.

The Spinning Heart

The fireflies and the stars our only light,
We rock, watching between the roses night
If we could see the roses. We cannot.
Where do the fireflies go by day, what eat?
What categories shall we use tonight?
The day was an exasperating day,
The day in history must hang its head
For the foul letters many women got,
Appointments missed, men dishevelled and sad
Before their mirrors trying to be proud.
But now (we say) the sweetness of the night
Will hide our imperfections from our sight,
For nothing can be angry or astray,
No man unpopular, lonely, or beset,
Where half a yellow moon hangs from a cloud.

Spinning however and balled up in space
All hearts, desires, pewter and honeysuckle,
What can be known of the individual face?
To the continual drum-beat of the blood
Mesh sea and mountain recollection, flame,
Motives in the corridor, touch by night,
Violent touch, and violence in rooms;
How shall we reconcile in any light
This blow and the relations that it wrecked?
Crescent the pressures on the singular act
Freeze it at last into its season, place,
Until the flood and disorder of Spring.

To Easterfield the court's best bore, defining
Space tied into a sailor's reef, our praise:
He too is useful, he is part of this,
Inimitable, tangible, post-human,
And Theo's disappointment has a place,
An item in that metamorphosis
The horrible coquetry of aging women.
Our superstitions barnacle our eyes
To the tide, the coming good; or has it come?—
Insufficient upon the beaches of the world
To drown that complex and that bestial drum.

Triumphant animal,—upon the rest
Bearing down hard, brooding, come to announce
The causes and directions of all this
Biting and breeding,—how will all your sons
Discover what you, assisted or alone,
Staring and sweating for seventy years,
Could never discover, the thing itself?
                                        Your fears,
Fidelity, and dandelions grown
As big as elephants, your morning lust
Can neither name nor control. No time for shame,
Whippoorwill calling, excrement falling, time
Rushes like a madman forward. Nothing can be known.

On the London Train

Despite the lonesome look
The man in the corner has,
Across the compartment,
Doubtless a dozen daze
Daily their eyes on him intent
And fancy him beside a brook,
Their arms with his laced,
Holding him fast.

Whilst he for some virgin
Endures the vacant night
Without rest, and would go
On bare knees, eyes shut tight,
To Tomsk or San Diego
If she'd but let him in,
Bind his hurt knees, or say
'There is a doctor down the way.'

So it is and has been . .
Summon an old lover's ghost,
He'll swear no man has lied
Who spoke of the painful and most
Embarrassing ordeal this side
Satisfaction,—while the green
Difficulties later are
More than Zeus could bear.

Austere in a sheltered place
The sea-shell puzzles Destiny,
Who set us, man and beast
And bird, in extremity

To love and twig a nest.
The frown on the great face
Is recompence too little for
Who suffer on the shore.

Caravan

The lady in her silver-
grey spectacular
Dressing-room prepares,
Twisting at the mirror,
Of son and daughter the careers.

Also in the evening
He who collects dung
Conjures an August moon
Where he may once bring
Her flushed and salt, supine.

The blue vase having final
Wit glitters fragile
Until at the horizon
To sky and sea all
Divides, throwing off season.

Thus kept delicately
In appalling storm the
Buds will begin again
Their white difficulty
To the mature and green.

Waves, guilt, all winter tears
Draw tingling nearer
And hang a glass for apparition . .
As the words here are
At work upon salvation.

The Possessed

This afternoon, discomfortable dead
Drift into doorways, lounge, across the bridge,
Whittling memory at the water's edge,
And watch. This is what you inherited.

Random they are, but hairy, for they chafe
All in their eye, enlarging like a slide;
Spectral as men once met or crucified,
And kind. Until the sun sets you are safe.

A prey to your most awkward reflection,
Loose-limbed before the fire you sit appalled
And think that by your error you have called
These to you. Look! the light will soon be gone.

Excited see from the window the men fade
In the twilight; reappear two doors down.
Suppose them well acquainted with the town
Who built it. Do you fumble in the shade?

The key was lost, remember, yesterday,
Or stolen,—undergraduates perhaps;
But all men are their colleagues, and eclipse
Very like dusk. It is too late to pray.

There was a time crepuscular was mild,
The hour for tea, acquaintances, and fall
Away of all day's difficulties, all
Discouragement. Weep, you are not a child.

The equine hour rears, no further friend,
Intolerant, foam-lathered, pregnant with
Mysterious grave watchers in their wrath
Let into tired Troy. You are near the end.

Midsummer Common loses its last gold,
And grey is there. The sun slants down behind
A certain cinema, and the world is blind
But more dangerous. It is growing cold.

Light all the lights, heap wood upon the fire
To banish shadow. Draw the curtains tight.
But sightless eyes will lean through, and wide night
Darken this room of yours. As you desire.

Think on your sins with all intensity.
The men are on the stair, they will not wait.
There is a paper-knife to penetrate
Heart & guilt together. Do it quickly.

Parting as Descent

The sun rushed up the sky; the taxi flew;
There was a kind of fever on the clock
That morning. We arrived at Waterloo
With time to spare and couldn't find my track.

The bitter coffee in a small café
Gave us our conversation. When the train
Began to move, I saw you turn away
And vanish, and the vessels in my brain

Burst, the train roared, the other travellers
In flames leapt, burning on the tilted air
Che si cruccia, I heard the devils curse
And shriek with joy in that place beyond prayer.

Cloud and Flame

The summer cloud in summer blue
Capricious from the wind will run,
Laughing into the tender sun,
Knowing the work that it must do.
When One says liberty is vain
The cloud will come to summer rain.

After his college failure, Swift
Eight hours a day against his age
Began to document his rage
Towards the decades of strife and shift.
From claims that pride or party made
He kept in an exacting shade.

Cornford in a retreat was lost;
A stray shot like an aimless joke
His learning, spirit, at one stroke
Dispersed, his generation's cost.
The harvest value of his head
Is less than cloud, is less than bread.

The One recalls the many burn,
Prepared or unprepared: one flame
Within a shade can strike its name,
Another sees the cloud return.
And Thirkill saw the Christ's head shake
At Hastings, by the Bloody Lake.

Letter to His Brother

The night is on these hills, and some can sleep.
Some stare into the dark, some walk.
Only the sound of glasses and of talk,
Of cracking logs, and of a few who weep,
Comes on the night wind to my waking ears.
Your enemies and mine are still,
None works upon us either good or ill:
Mint by the stream, tree-frogs, are travellers.

What shall I say for anniversary?
At Dachau rubber blows forbid
And Becket's brains upon the pavement spread
Forbid my trust, my hopeful prophecy.
Prediction if I make, I violate
The just expectancy of youth,—
Although you know as well as I whose tooth
Sunk in our heels, the western guise of fate.

When Patrick Barton chased the murderer
He heard behind him in the wood
Pursuit, and suddenly he knew hé fled:
He was the murderer, the others were
His vigilance. But when he crouched behind
A tree, the tree moved off and left
Him naked while the cry came on; he laughed
And like a hound he leapt out of his mind.

I wish for you—the moon was full, is gone—
Whatever bargain can be got
From the violent world our fathers bought,
For which we pay with fantasy at dawn,

Dismay at noon, fatigue, horror by night.
May love, or its image in work,
Bring you the brazen luck to sleep with dark
And so to get responsible delight.

1938

Desires of Men and Women

Exasperated, worn, you conjure a mansion,
The absolute butlers in the spacious hall,
Old silver, lace, and privacy, a house
Where nothing has for years been out of place,
Neither shoe-horn nor affection been out of place,
Breakfast in summer on the eastern terrace,
All justice and all grace.

                              At the reception
Most beautifully you conduct yourselves—
Expensive and accustomed, bow, speak French,
That Cinquecento miniature recall
The Duke presented to your great-grandmother—

And none of us, my dears, would dream of you
The half-lit and lascivious apartments
That are in fact your goal, for which you'd do
Murder if you had not your cowardice
To prop the law; or dream of you the rooms,
Glaring and inconceivably vulgar,
Where now you are, where now you wish for life,
Whence you project your naked fantasies.

World-Telegram

Man with a tail heads eastward for the Fair.
Can open a pack of cigarettes with it.
Was weaving baskets happily, it seems,
When found, the almost Missing Link, and brought
From Ceylon in the interests of science.
The correspondent doesn't know how old.

Two columns left, a mother saw her child
Crushed with its father by a ten-ton truck
Against a loading platform, while her son,
Small, frightened, in a Sea Scout uniform,
Watched from the Langley. All needed treatment.

Berlin and Rome are having difficulty
With a new military pact. Some think
Russia is not too friendly towards London.
The British note is called inadequate.

An Indian girl in Lima, not yet six,
Has been delivered by Caesarian.
A boy. They let the correspondent in:
Shy, uncommunicative, still quite pale,
A holy picture by her, a blue ribbon.

Right of the centre, and three columns wide,
A rather blurred but rather ominous
Machine-gun being set up by militia
This morning in Harlan County, Kentucky.
Apparently some miners died last night.
'Personal brawls' is the employers' phrase.

All this on the front page. Inside, penguins.
The approaching television of baseball.
The King approaching Quebec. Cotton down.
Skirts up. Four persons shot. Advertisements.
Twenty-six policemen are decorated.
Mother's Day repercussions. A film star
Hopes marriage will preserve him from his fans.

News of one day, one afternoon, one time.
If it were possible to take these things
Quite seriously, I believe they might
Curry disorder in the strongest brain,
Immobilize the most resilient will,
Stop trains, break up the city's food supply,
And perfectly demoralize the nation.

11 MAY 1939

Conversation

Whether the moorings are invisible
Or slipt, we said we could not tell,
But argument held one thing sure
Which none of us that night could well endure:
The ship is locked with fog, no man aboard
Can make out what he's moving toward,
There's little food, few love, less sleep,
The sea is dark and we are told it's deep.

Where is an officer who knows this coast?
If all such men long since have faced
Downward, one summon. Who knows how,
With what fidelity, his voice heard now
Could shout directions from the ocean's floor?
Traditional characters no more
Their learnéd simple parts rehearse
But bed them softly down from the time's curse.

A snapt short log pitched out upon the hearth,
The flaming harbinger come forth
Of holocausts that night and day
Flake from the mind its skinny sovereignty.
We watched the embers cool, embers that brought
To one man there the failing thought
Of cities stripped of knowledge, men,
Our continent a wilderness again.

These are conclusions of the night, we said;
And drank; and were not satisfied.
The fire died down, smoke in the air
Assumed the alarming postures of our fear,—

The overhead horror, in the padded room
The man who will not tell his name,
The guns and subtle friends who face
Into this delicate and dangerous place.

1938

Ancestor

The old men wept when the Old Man in blue
Bulked in the doorway of the train, Time spun
And in that instant's revolution Time
(Who cannot love old men) dealt carelessly
Passions and shames upon his hardihood,
Seeing the wet eyes of his former staff:

Crossing from Tennessee, the river at flood,
White River Valley, his original regiment,
The glowflies winking in the gully's dusk,
Three horses shot from under him at Shiloh
Fell, the first ball took Hindman's horse as well
And then the two legs from an orderly

Rain on the lost field, mire and violence,
Corruption; Klan-talk, half-forgotten tongue
Rubbed up for By-Laws and its Constitution,
The Roman syllables'
                 he an exile fled,
Both his plantations, great-grandmother's too
Gone, fled south and south into Honduras
Where great-grandmother was never reconciled
To monkeys or the thought of monkeys
                         once
Tricked into taking bites of one, she kept
Eight months her bed
                 fire on the colony,
Lifting of charges, and a late return,
The stranger in his land, and silence, silence . .

(Only the great grey riddled cloak spoke out
And sometimes a sudden breath or look spoke out)
Reflecting blue saw in the tears of men,
The tyrant shade, shade of the last of change,
And coughed once, twice, massive and motionless;
Now Federal, now Sheriff, near four-score,
Controlled with difficulty his old eyes
As he stepped down, for the first time, in blue.

World's Fair

The crowd moves forward on the midway, back
And forward, men and women from every State
Insisting on their motion like a clock.
I stand by the roller-coaster, and wait.
An hour I have waited, fireworks on the lake
Tell me it's late, and yet it is not that
Which rattles at the bottom of my mind,
Slight, like a faint sound sleepy on the wind
To the traveller when he has lost his track.

Suddenly in torn images I trace
The inexhaustible ability of a man
Loved once, long lost, still to prevent my peace,
Still to suggest my dreams and starve horizon.
Childhood speaks to me in an austere face.
The Chast Mayd only to the thriving Swan
Looks back and back with lecherous intent,
Being the one nail known, an excrement;
Middleton's grave in a forgotten place.

That recognition fades now, and I stand
Exhausted, angry, beside the wooden rail
Where tireless couples mount still, hand in hand,
For the complex drug of catapult and fall
To blot out the life they cannot understand
And never will forgive. The wind is stale,
The crowd thins, and my friend has not yet come.
It is long past midnight, time to track for home
And my work and the instructor down my mind.

Travelling South

A red moon hung above the pines that night
Travelling, as we travelled, south. First one,
Then two, streamers of cloud across the moon
Crept and trivided the cold brooding light
Like blood. The captive hum under the hood
Pacing, the pebbles plunging, throbbing mind
Raced through the night, afraid of what we'd find
For brother at the end, sightless or dead.

The same womb bore us. What is the time of man?
At what time does he rise and go to bed?
When shall a young man bend his hopeful head
Upon the block, under a red red moon,
And lose that dear head? I was dull with fear,
The car devoured the darkness, the moon hung,
Blood over the pines, and the cold wind sang
Welcome, welcome the executioner.

O then the lighted house, the nurse, at last
Painfully but his real face, his hand
Moving, his voice to melt the frozen wind;
Trouble but trouble that would soon be past;
Injury, but salvation. The headsman stood
Once at the block, looked on the young man stark,
And let that young man rise. In the flowing dark
The pines consumed the moon and the moon of blood.

At Chinese Checkers

I

Again—but other faces bend with mine
Upon the board—I settle to this game
And drive my marbles leaping or in line
Towards the goal, the triangular blue aim
Of all my red ones, as it was before.
Sitting with strangers by a Northern lake
I watch the opening and the shutting door,
The paradigms shift and break.

II

The table moves before my restless eyes,
Part of an oak, an occupation once,
This town humming with men and lumber, cries,
Will, passionate activity that since
Dwindled, died when the woods cut without plan
Were thirty years ago exhausted. Now
The jackpine where the locomotive ran
Springs up wild; the docks are rotten with snow.

III

Last night for the first time I saw the Lights,
The folding of the Lights like upright cloud
Swinging as, in a childhood summer, kites
Swung, and the boys who owned the kites were proud.
What pride was active in that gorgeous sky?
What dreadful leniency compelled the men
Southward, the crumpled men? Questions went by,
Swung in the dark back and were gone again.

IV

Far on the dunes the wind is rising, sand
Drifts with it, drops; under the rounding moon
Deer, hesitating from the wood, will stand
Until their promise is a lonely dune
And they come forward, masters for the time
Of all that mountainous dead world, cold light.
The glittering rocks are naked as a tomb
Where the sea was; alteration is the night.

V

Insistent voices recall me to the play.
I triple over blue and yellow, sit
Erect and smile; but what it is they say
My ears will not accept, I mangle it,
I see their faces change, I hear the wind
Begin to whistle under the shut door,
The door shudders, I cannot hold my mind,
Backward, east, south it goes in the wind's roar.

VI

I am again in the low and country room
Where all that is was heart-wrung, had by hard
Continual labour. We are at the game:
Excited childish cries over the board,
The old man grumbling in the darkness there
Beside the stove, Baynard is still, intent,
And to my left his sister has her chair,
Her great eyes to the flashing marbles bent.

VII

The shy head and the delicate throat conceal
A voice that even undisciplined can stir

The country blood over a Southern hill.
Will Ingreet's voice bring her renown, bring her
That spontaneous acclaim an artist needs
Unless he works in the solitary dark?
What prophecy, what hope can older heads
Proclaim, beyond the exhaustion of the work?

VIII

How shall we counsel the unhappy young
Or young excited in their thoughtlessness
By game or deviltry or popular song?
Too many, blazing like disease, confess
In their extinction the consuming fear
No man has quite escaped: the good, the wise,
The masters of their generation, share
This pressure of inaction on their eyes.

IX

I move the white, jumping the red and green,
Blue if I can, to finish where the blue
Marbles before they issued forth began,
And fill the circles, as I ought to do.
Can I before the children win that place?
Their energies are here at work, not mine:
The beautiful absorption on Sue's face
My crowded travelling face cannot design.

X

The fox-like child I was or assume I was
I lose, the abstract remember only; all
The lightness and the passion for running lose
Together with all my terror, the blind call
At midnight for the mother. How shall we know

The noon we are to be in night we are?
The altering winds are dark and the winds blow
Agitation and rest, unclear, unclear.

XI

Deep in the unfriendly city Delmore lies
And cannot sleep, and cannot bring his mind
And cannot bring those marvellous faculties
To bear upon the day sunk down behind,
The unsteady night, or the time to come.
Slack the large frame, he sprawls upon his bed
Useless, the eloquent mouth relaxed and dumb,
Trouble and mist in the apathetic head.

XII

What prophecies, what travel? Strangers call
Across the miles of table, and I return,
Bewildered, see burnt faces rise and fall
In the recapitulation of their urn.
I speak; all of us laugh; the game goes on.
The Northern wind is moaning still outside.
The sense of change, suns gone up and come down,
Whirls in my tired head, and it will abide.

XIII

Against my will once in another game
I spat a piece of tooth out—this was love
Or the innocence of love, long past its time
Virgin with trust, which time makes nothing of.
The wind is loud. I wonder, Will it grow,
That trust, again? Can it again be strong?
What rehabilitations can the heart know
When the heart is split, when the faithful heart is wrong?

XIV

Venus on the half-shell was found a dish
To madden a fanatic: from the nave
Rolled obloquy and lust. Sea without fish,
Flat sea, and Simonetta had a grave
Deeper than the dark cliff of any tooth,
Deeper than memory. Obstinate, malicious,
The man across the table shouts an oath,
The sea recedes, strangers possess the house.

XV

Marbles are not the marbles that they were,
The accurate bright knuckle-breakers boys
In alleys, where there is no one to care,
Use, in the schoolyard use at noon, and poise
As Pheidias his incomparable gold.
The gold is lost. But issued from the tomb,
Delmore's magical tongue. What the sea told
Will keep these violent strangers from our room.

XVI

The marbles of the blood drive to their place,
Foam in the heart's level. The heart will mend,
Body will break and mend, the foam replace
For even the unconsolable his taken friend.
Wind is the emblem of the marbles' rest,
The sorrowful, the courageous marble's hurt
And strange recovery. Stubborn in the breast
The break and ache, the plunging powerful heart.

1939

The Animal Trainer (1)

I told him: The time has come, I must be gone.
It is time to leave the circus and circus days,
The admissions, the menagerie, the drums,
Excitements of disappointment and praise.
In a suburb of the spirit I shall seize
The steady and exalted light of the sun,
And live there, out of the tension that decays,
Until I become a man alone of noon.

Heart said: Can you do without your animals?
The looking, licking, smelling animals?
The friendly fumbling beast? The listening one?
That standing up and worst of animals?
What will become of you in the pure light
When all your enemies are gone, and gone
The inexhaustible prospect of the night?

—But the night is now the body of my fear,
These animals are my distraction. Once
Let me escape the smells and cages here,
Once let me stand naked in the sun,
All these performances will be forgotten.
I shall concentrate in the sunlight there.

Said the conservative Heart: Your animals
Are occupation, food for you, your love
And your immense responsibility;
They are the travellers by which you live.
(Without you they will pace and pine, or die.)

—I reared them, tended them (I said) and still
They plague me, they will not perform, they run
Into forbidden corners, they fight, they steal.
Better to live like an artist in the sun.

—You are an animal trainer, Heart replied.
Without your animals leaping at your side
No sun will save you, nor this bloodless pride.

—What must I do then? Must I stay and work
With animals, and confront the night, in the circus?

—You léarn from animals. You léarn in the dark.

The Animal Trainer (2)

I told him: The time has come, I must be gone.
It is time to leave the circus and circus days,
The admissions, the menagerie, the drums,
Excitements of disappointment and praise.
In a suburb of the spirit I shall seize
The steady and exalted light of the sun
And live there, out of the tension that decays,
Until I become a man alone of noon.

Heart said: Can you do without these animals?
The looking, licking, smelling animals?
The friendly fumbling beast? The listening one?
The standing up and worst of animals?
What will become of you in the pure light
When all your enemies are gone, and gone
The inexhaustible prospect of the night?

—But the night is now the body of my fear,
These animals are my distraction! Once
Let me escape the smells and cages here,
Once let me stand naked in the sun,
All their performances will be forgotten.
I shall concentrate in the sunlight there.

Said the conservative Heart: These animals
Are occupation, food for you, your love
And your despair, responsibility:
They are the travellers by which you live.
Without you they will pace and pine, or die.

—What soul-delighting tasks do they perform?
They quarrel, snort, leap, lie down, their delight
Merely a punctual meal and to be warm.
Justify their existence in the night!

—The animals are coupling, and they cry
'The circus *is*, it is our mystery,
It is a world of dark where animals die.'

—Animals little and large, be still, be still:
I'll stay with you. Suburb and sun are pale.

—Animals are your destruction, and your will.

III

1 *September* 1939

The first, scattering rain on the Polish cities.
That afternoon a man squat' on the shore
Tearing a square of shining cellophane.
Some easily, some in evident torment tore,
Some for a time resisted, and then burst.
All this depended on fidelity . .
One was blown out and borne off by the waters,
The man was tortured by the sound of rain.

Children were sent from London in the morning
But not the sound of children reached his ear.
He found a mangled feather by the lake,
Lost in the destructive sand this year
Like feathery independence, hope. His shadow
Lay on the sand before him, under the lake
As under the ruined library our learning.
The children play in the waves until they break.

The Bear crept under the Eagle's wing and lay
Snarling; the other animals showed fear,
Europe darkened its cities. The man wept,
Considering the light which had been there,
The feathered gull against the twilight flying.
As the little waves ate away the shore
The cellophane, dismembered, blew away.
The animals ran, the Eagle soared and dropt.

Desire Is a World by Night

The history of strangers in their dreams
Being irresponsible, is fun for men,
Whose sons are neither at the Front nor frame
Humiliating weakness to keep at home
Nor wince on principle, wearing mother grey,
Honoured by radicals. When the mind is free
The catechetical mind can mince and tear
Contemptible vermin from a stranger's hair
And then sleep.

          In our parents' dreams we see
Vigour abutting on senility,
Stiff blood, and weathered with the years, poor vane;
Unfortunate but inescapable.
Although this wind bullies the windowpane
Are the children to be kept responsible
For the world's decay? Carefully we choose
Our fathers, carefully we cut out those
On whom to exert the politics of praise.

Heard after dinner, in defenceless ease,
The dreams of friends can puzzle, dazzle us
With endless journeys through unfriendly snow,
Malevolent faces that appear and frown
Where nothing was expected, the sudden stain
On spotless window-ledges; these we take
Chuckling, but take them with us when we go,
To study in secret, late, brooding, looking
For trails and parallels. We have a stake
In this particular region, and we look
Excitedly for situations that we know.

—The disinterested man has gone abroad;
Winter is on the by-way where he rode
Erect and alone, summery years ago.

When we dream, paraphrase, analysis
Exhaust the crannies of the night. We stare,
Fresh sweat upon our foreheads, as they fade:
The melancholy and terror of avenues
Where long no single man has moved, but play
Under the arc-lights gangs of the grey dead
Running directionless. That bright blank place
Advances with us into fearful day,
Heady and insuppressible. Call in friends,
They grin and carry it carefully away,—
The fathers can't be trusted,—strangers wear
Their strengths, and visor. Last, authority,
The Listener borrow from an English grave
To solve our hatred and our bitterness . .
The foul and absurd to solace or dismay.
All this will never appear; we will not say;
Let the evidence be buried in a cave
Off the main road. If anyone could see
The white scalp of that passionate will and those
Sullen desires, he would stumble, dumb,
Retreat into the time from which he came
Counting upon his fingers and his toes.

Farewell to Miles

We are to tell one man tonight good-bye.
Therefore in little glasses Scotch, therefore
Inane talk on the chaise longue by the door,
Therefore the loud man, the man small and shy
Who squats, the hostess as she has a nut
Laughing like ancestor. Hard, hard to find
In thirteen bodies one appropriate mind,
It is hard to find a knife that we can cut.

The dog is wandering among the men
And wander may: who knows where who will be,
Under what master, in what company,
When what we hope for has not come again
For the last time? Schedules, nerves will crack
In the distortion of that ultimate loss;
Sad eyes at frenzied eyes will look across,
Blink, be resigned. The men then will come back.

How many of these are destined there? Not one
But may be there, staring; but some may trick
By attack or by some prodigy of luck
The sly dog. McPherson in the Chinese sun
May achieve the annihilation of his will;
The urbane and bitter Miles at Harvard may
Discover in time an acid holiday
And let the long wound of his birth lie still.

Possibilities, dreams, in a crowded room.
Fantasy for the academic man,
Release, distinction. Let the man who can,
Does any peace know, now arise and come

Out of the highballs, past the dog, forward.
(I hope you will be happier where you go
Than you or we were here, and learn to know
What satisfactions there are.) No one heard.

WAYNE, *1940*

The Moon and the Night and the Men

On the night of the Belgian surrender the moon rose
Late, a delayed moon, and a violent moon
For the English or the American beholder;
The French beholder. It was a cold night,
People put on their wraps, the troops were cold
No doubt, despite the calendar, no doubt
Numbers of refugees coughed, and the sight
Or sound of some killed others. A cold night.

On Outer Drive there was an accident:
A stupid well-intentioned man turned sharp
Right and abruptly he became an angel
Fingering an unfamiliar harp,
Or screamed in hell, or was nothing at all.
Do not imagine this is unimportant.
He was a part of the night, part of the land,
Part of the bitter and exhausted ground
Out of which memory grows.

              Michael and I
Stared at each other over chess, and spoke
As little as possible, and drank and played.
The chessmen caught in the European eye,
Neither of us I think had a free look
Although the game was fair. The move one made
It was difficult at last to keep one's mind on.
'Hurt and unhappy' said the man in London.
We said to each other, The time is coming near
When none shall have books or music, none his dear,
And only a fool will speak aloud his mind.
History is approaching a speechless end,
As Henry Adams said. Adams was right.

All this occurred on the night when Leopold
Fulfilled the treachery four years before
Begun—or was he well-intentioned, more
Roadmaker to hell than king? At any rate,
The moon came up late and the night was cold,
Many men died—although we know the fate
Of none, nor of anyone, and the war
Goes on, and the moon in the breast of man is cold.

White Feather

(AFTER A NEWS ITEM)

Imagine a crowded war-time street
Down Under. See as little as I:
The woman gives him as they meet
Passing, something . . a feather. Try
To make out this man who was going by.
The eye stared at the feather.

He could remember sand and sand,
The punishing sun on their guns; he chose
As the men approached the western end
To move to the left. Who would suppose
A Lieutenant in civilian clothes?
The feather stared back.

He dropt his glass eye in her hand.
. . Humiliation or fantasy,
He thought; I have seen too much sand
For judgment or anger; it may be I,
All men, deserve the feather's lie.
The eye stared at the feather.

The Enemies of the Angels

I

The Irish and the Italians own the place.
Anyone owns it, if you like, who has
A dollar minimum; but it is theirs by noise.
Let them possess it until one o'clock,
The balconies' tiers, huddled tables, shroud-
ed baleful music, and the widening crack
Across the far wall watching a doomed crowd,
The fat girl simpering carnations to the boys.

This is a paradise the people seek,
To hide, if they but knew, being awake,
Losses and crisis. This is where they come
For love, for fun, to forget, dance, to conceal
Their slow perplexity by the river. Who
But pities the kissing couple? Who would feel
Disdain, as she does, being put on show
By whom she loves? And pity . . our images of home.

The arrival of the angels is delayed
An even minute, and I am afraid
We clapped because they fail to, not because
They come. Their wings are sorry. The platform
A little shudders as they back and frisk,
We'd maul the angels, the whole room is warm,—
A waste, and a creation without risk;
Jostling, pale as they vanish, the horse-faced chorine paws.

The impersonator is our special joy
And puzzle: did the nurse announce a boy
Or not? But now the guy is all things, all

Women and most men howl when he takes off
Our President, the Shadow, Garbo or Bing
And other marvellous persons. "Sister Rough"
The sailors at their table, gesturing,
Soprano, whistling. Still, recall him, and recall

Mimics we wish we all were, and we are.
We lack a subject just, we lack a car,
We would see two Mayors bowing as we pass,
We wish we had another suit, we wish
Another chance, we would have Western life
Where the hero reins and fans, horseflesh is flesh.
But the heckling man and his embarrassed wife
Play us across the mirrored room. Where is my glass?

II

My tall and singular friend two feet away,
Where do you go at the end of another day?
What is your lot, your wife's lot, under the Lord?
If you between two certain ages, more
Nor less, are, and if you revere the Flag
Or whether, Friend, you find a flag a bore
And whether Democracy blooms or you see it sag,
What is your order number at your Local Board?

Where do you all go? Not with whom you would;
But where you went as little boys, when good,
To the plains' heaven of the silver screen.
This comic in a greatcoat is your will,
The faery presence walking among men
Who mock him: sly, baffled, and powerful

For imagination is his, and imagination
Ruins, compels; consider the comedian again.

The orchestra returns and tunes before
A spot, a flash, the M.C. through the door
Glides like a breakfast to your vision—gay
Indelicate intimate, "Jerk, what do you know?"
An aging, brimstone acrobat in pink
Monkeys her way across the blue boards. Who
Resists her? Who would be unkind to think
A human wheel, a frozen smile, is human woe?

Consider, students, at the convalescent hour
The fantasy which last week you saw fair,
Which loses now its eye; its eye is gone.
Where shall the ten be found to safe us? For
The enemies of the angels, hard on sleep,
Weary themselves to find the Gentlemen's door.
It is not a little one. Perhaps you weep,
Three eyes weep in the world you inhabit alone.

All this resist. Who wish their stays away
Or wish them tighter tighter—the mourners pray
In narrowing circles—these are women lost,
Are men lost in the drag of women's eyes,
Salt mouths. Go with the tide, at midnight dream
Hecklers will vanish like a radical's lies,
And all Life slides from drink to drink, the stream
Slides, and under the stream we join a happy ghost.

A Poem for Bhain

Although the relatives in the summer house
Gossip and grumble, do what relatives do,
Demand, demand our eyes and ears, demand us,

You and I are not precisely there
As they require: heretics, we converse
Alert and alone, as over a lake of fire

Two white birds following their profession
Of flight, together fly, loom, fall and rise,
Certain of the nature and station of their mission.

So by the superficial and summer lake
We talk, and nothing that we say is heard,
Neither by the relatives who twitter and ache

Nor by any traveller nor by any bird.

Boston Common
A *Meditation upon The Hero*

I
Slumped under the impressive genitals
Of the bronze charger, protected by bronze,
By darkness from patrols, by sleep from what
Assailed him earlier and left him here,
The man lies. Clothing and organs. These were once
Shoes. Faint in the orange light
Flooding the portico above: the whole
Front of the State House. On a February night.

II
Dramatic bivouac for the casual man!
Beyond the exedra the Common falls,
Famous and dark, away; a lashing wind;
Immortal heroes in a marble frame
Who broke their bodies on Fort Wagner's walls,
Robert Gould Shaw astride, and his
Negroes without name, who followed, who fell
Screaming or calm, wet cold, sick or oblivious.

III
Who now cares how? here they are in their prime,—
Paradigm, pitching imagination where
The crucible night all singularity,
Idiosyncrasy and creed, burnt out
And brought them, here, a common character.
Imperishable march below
The mounted man below the Angel, and
Under, the casual man, the possible hero.

IV

Hero for whom under a sky of bronze,
Saint-Gaudens' sky? Passive he seems to lie,
The last straw of contemporary thought,
In shapeless failure; but may be this man
Before he came here, or he comes to die,
Blazing with force or fortitude
Superb of civil soul may stand or may
After young Shaw within that crucible have stood.

V

For past her assignation when night fell
And the men forward,—poise and shock of dusk
As daylight rocking passes the horizon,—
The Angel spread her wings still. War is the
Congress of adolescents, love in a mask,
Bestial and easy, issueless,
Or gets a man of bronze. No beating heart
Until the casual man can see the Angel's face.

VI

Where shall they meet? what ceremony find,
Loose in the brothel of another war
This winter night? Can citizen enact
His timid will and expectation where,
Exact a wedding or her face O where
Tanks and guns, tanks and guns,
Move and must move to their conclusions, where
The will is mounted and gregarious and bronze?

VII

For ceremony, in the West, in the East,
The pierced sky, iced air, and the rent of cloud

As, moving to his task at dawn, who'd been
Hobbledehoy of the cafeteria life
Swung like a hobby in the blue and rode
The shining body of his choice
To the eye and time of his bombardier;—
Stiffened in the racket, and relaxed beyond noise.

VIII

'Who now cares how?'—the quick, the index! Question
Your official heroes in a magazine,
Wry voices past the river. Dereliction,
Lust and bloodlust, error and goodwill, this one
Died howling, craven, this one was a swine
From childhood. Man and animal
Sit for their photographs to Fame, and dream
Barbershop hours . . vain, compassionate parable.

IX

"Accidents of history, memorials"—
A considering and quiet voice. "I see
Photograph and bronze upon another shore
Do not arrive; the light is where it is,
Indifferent to honour. Let honour be
Consolation to those who give,
None to the Hero, and no sign of him:
All unrecorded, flame-like, perish and live."

X

Diminishing beyond the elms. Rise now
The chivalry and defenders of our time,
From Spain and China, the tortured continents,
Leningrad, Syria, Corregidor,—

Upon a primitive theme high variations
Like soaring Beethoven's.—Lost, lost
Whose eyes flung faultless to one horizon
Their fan look. Fiery night consumes a summoned
  ghost.

XI

Images of the Possible, the top,
Their time they taxed,—after the tanks came through,
When orderless and by their burning homes'
Indelible light, with knee and nail they struck
(The improvised the real) man's common foe,
Misled blood-red statistical men.
Images of conduct in a crucible,
Their eyes, and nameless eyes, which will not come
  again.

XII

We hope will not again. Therefore those eyes
Fix me again upon the terrible shape,
Defeated and marvellous, of the man I know,
Jack under the stallion. We have passed him by,
Wandering, prone, and he is our whole hope,
Our fork's one time and our despair,
The heart of the Future beating. How far far
We sent our subtle messengers! when he is here.

XIII

Who chides our clamour and who would forget
The death of heroes: never know the shore
Where, hair to the West, Starkatterus was burnt;
And undergo no more that spectacle—

Perpetually verdant the last pyre,
Fir, cypress, yew, the phoenix bay
And voluntary music—which to him
Threw never meat or truth. He looks another way,

XIV

Watching who labour O that all may see
And savour the blooming world, flower and sound,
Tending and tending to peace,—be what their blood,
Prayer, occupation may,—so tend for all:
A common garden in a private ground.
Who labour in the private dark
And silent dark for birthday music and light,
Fishermen, gardeners, about their violent work.

XV

Lincoln, the lanky lonely and sad man
Who suffered in Washington his own, his soul;
Mao Tse-Tung, Teng Fa, fabulous men,
Laughing and serious men; or Tracy Doll
Tracing the future on the wall of a cell—
There, there, on the wall of a cell
The face towards which we hope all history,
Institutions, tears move, there the Individual.

XVI

Ah, it may not be so. Still the crucial night
Fastens you all upon this frame of hope:
Each in his limited sick world with them,
The figures of his reverence, his awe,
His shivering devotion,—that they shape
Shelter, action, salvation.

. . Legends and lies. Kneel if you will, but rise
Homeless, alone, and be the kicking working one.

XVII
None anywhere alone! The turning world
Brings unaware us to our enemies,
Artist to assassin, Saint-Gaudens' bronze
To a free shelter, images to end.
The cold and hard wind has tears in my eyes,
Long since, long since, I heard the last
Traffic unmeshing upon Boylston Street,
I halted here in the orange light of the Past,

XVIII
Helpless under the great crotch lay this man
Huddled against woe, I had heard defeat
All day, I saw upon the sands assault,
I heard the voice of William James, the wind,
And poured in darkness or in my heartbeat
Across my hearing and my sight
Worship and love irreconcilable
Here to be reconciled. On a February night.

1942

IV

Canto Amor

Dream in a dream the heavy soul somewhere
struck suddenly & dark down to its knees.
A griffin sighs off in the orphic air.

If (Unknown Majesty) I not confess
praise for the wrack the rock the live sailor
under the blue sea,—yet I may You bless

always for hér, in fear & joy for hér
whose gesture summons ever when I grieve
me back and is my mage and minister.

—Muses: whose worship I may never leave
but for this pensive woman, now I dare,
teach me her praise! with her my praise receive.—

Three years already of the round world's war
had rolled by stoned & disappointed eyes
when she and I came where we were made for.

Pale as a star lost in returning skies,
more beautiful than midnight stars more frail
she moved towards me like chords, a sacrifice;

entombed in body trembling through the veil
arm upon arm, learning our ancient wound,
we see our one soul heal, recovering pale.

Then priestly sanction, then the drop of sound.
Quickly part to the cavern ever warm
deep from the march, body to body bound,

descend (my soul) out of dismantling storm
into the darkness where the world is made.
. . Come back to the bright air. Love is multiform.

Heartmating hesitating unafraid
although incredulous, she seemed to fill
the lilac shadow with light wherein she played,

whom sorry childhood had made sit quite still,
an orphan silence, unregarded sheen,
listening for any small soft note, not hopeful:

caricature: as once a maiden Queen,
flowering power comeliness kindness grace,
shattered her mirror, wept, would not be seen.

These pities moved. Also above her face
serious or flushed, swayed her fire-gold
not earthly hair, now moonless to unlace,

resistless flame, now in a sun more cold
great shells to whorl about each secret ear,
mysterious histories, white shores, unfold.

New musics! One the music that we hear,
this is the music which the masters make
out of their minds, profound solemn & clear.

And then the other music, in whose sake
all men perceive a gladness but we are drawn
less for that joy than utterly to take

our trial, naked in the music's vision,
the flowing ceremony of trouble and light,
all Loves becoming, none to flag upon.

Such Mozart made,—an ear so delicate
he fainted at a trumpet-call, a child
so delicate. So merciful that sight,

so stern, we follow rapt who ran a-wild.
Marriage is the second music, and thereof
we hear what we can bear, faithful & mild.

Therefore the streaming torches in the grove
through dark or bright, swiftly & now more near
cherish a festival of anxious love.

Dance for this music, Mistress to music dear,
more, that storm worries the disordered wood
grieving the midnight of my thirtieth year

and only the trial of our music should
still this irresolute air, only your voice
spelling the tempest may compel our good:

Sigh then beyond my song: whirl & rejoice!

THE NERVOUS SONGS

Young Woman's Song

The round and smooth, my body in my bath,
If someone else would like it too.—I did,
I wanted T. to think 'How interesting'
Although I hate his voice and face, hate both.
I hate this something like a bobbing cork
Not going. I want something to hang to.—

A fierce wind roaring high up in the bare
Branches of trees,—I suppose it was lust
But it was holy and awful. All day I thought
I am a bobbing cork, irresponsible child
Loose on the waters.—What have you done at last?
A little work, a little vague chat.

I want that £3.10 hat terribly.—
What I am looking for (*I am*) may be
Happening in the gaps of what I know.
The full moon does go with you as yóu go.
Where am I going? I am not afraid . .
Only I would be lifted lost in the flood.

The Song of the Demented Priest

I put those things there.—See them burn.
The emerald the azure and the gold
Hiss and crack, the blues & greens of the world
As if I were tired. Someone interferes
Everywhere with me. The clouds, the clouds are torn
In ways I do not understand or love.

Licking my long lips, I looked upon God
And he flamed and he was friendlier
Than you were, and he was small. Showing me
Serpents and thin flowers; these were cold.
Dominion waved & glittered like the flare
From ice under a small sun. I wonder.

Afterward the violent and formal dancers
Came out, shaking their pithless heads.
I would instruct them but I cannot now,—
Because of the elements. They rise and move,
I nod a dance and they dance in the rain
In my red coat. I am the king of the dead.

The Song of the Young Hawaiian

Ai, they all pass in front of me those girls!
Blazing and lazy colours. The swaying sun
Brushes the brown tips of them stiffly softly
And whispers me: Never take only one
As the yellow men the white the foreigners do.—
No no, I dance them all.

The old men come to me at dusk and say
'Hang from their perches now the ruined birds;
They will fall. We hear strange languages.
Rarely a child sings now.' They cough and say
'We are a dying race.' Ai! if we are!
You will not marry me.

Strengthless the tame will of the elders' eyes.—
The green palms, the midnight sand, the creaming surf!
The sand at streaming noon is black. I swim
Farther than others, for I swim alone.
. . (Whom Nangganangga smashed to pieces on
The road to Paradise.)

A *Professor's Song*

(. . rabid or dog-dull.) Let me tell you how
The Eighteenth Century couplet ended. Now
Tell me. Troll me the sources of that Song—
Assigned last week—by Blake. Come, come along,
Gentlemen. (Fidget and huddle, do. Squint soon.)
I want to end these fellows all by noon.

'That deep romantic chasm'—an early use;
The word is from the French, by our abuse
Fished out a bit. (Red all your eyes. O when?)
'A poet is a man speaking to men':
But I am then a poet, am I not?—
Ha ha. The radiator, please. Well, what?

Alive now—no—Blake would have written prose,
But movement following movement crisply flows,
So much the better, better the much so,
As burbleth Mozart. Twelve. The class can go.
Until I meet you, then, in Upper Hell
Convulsed, foaming immortal blood: farewell.

The Captain's Song

The tree before my eyes bloomed into flame,
I rode the flame. This was the element,
Forsaking wife and child, I came to find,—
The flight through arrowy air dark as a dream
Brightening and falling, the loose tongues blue
Like blood above me, until I forgot.

. . Later, forgetting, I became a child
And fell down without reason and played games
Running, being the fastest, before dark
And often cried. Certain things I hid
That I had never liked, I leapt the stream
No one else could and darted off alone . .

You crippled Powers, cluster to me now:
Baffle this memory from my return,
That in the coldest nights, murmuring her name
I sought her two feet with my feet, my feet
Were warm and hers were ice and I warmed her
With both of mine. Will I warm her with one?

The Song of the Tortured Girl

After a little I could not have told—
But no one asked me this—why I was there.
I asked. The ceiling of that place was high
And there were sudden noises, which I made.
I must have stayed there a long time today:
My cup of soup was gone when they brought me back.

Often "Nothing worse now can come to us"
I thought, the winter the young men stayed away,
My uncle died, and mother broke her crutch.
And then the strange room where the brightest light
Does not shine on the strange men: shines on me.
I feel them stretch my youth and throw a switch.

Through leafless branches the sweet wind blows
Making a mild sound, softer than a moan;
High in a pass once where we put our tent,
Minutes I lay awake to hear my joy.
—I no longer remember what they want.—
Minutes I lay awake to hear my joy.

The Song of the Bridegroom

A sort of anxiousness crystal in crystal has . .
Fragile and open like these pairs of eyes.
All over all things move to stare at it.
One's single wish now: to be laid away
Felted in depths of caves, dark cupboards that
No one would open for a long time.—

Do not approach me! If I am on show
Compassion waves you past, you hoverers,
Forms brutal, beating eyes upon my window,
Because if I am desolate I have—
Have emanations, and it is not safe.
Rising and falling fire, ceremonial fire.

Not long . . not long but like a journey home
Frightening after so distant years
And such despairs . . And then fatigue sets in.
Lead me up blindly now where I began,
I will not wince away into my one.
I extend my hand and place it in the womb.

Song of the Man Forsaken and Obsessed

Viridian and gamboge and vermilion
Are and are not.—The hut is quiet,
Indistinct as letters. When I wake I wait.
Nothing comes.—The brown girl brings me rice
And one day months ago I might have stood—
So far were firm my feet—had that ship come—
And painted, softening my brush with blood.

Hardly, whatever happens from today.
—Certainly the little old woman
With a white eye, who takes all things away,
Comes and stares from the corner of my bed
If I could turn. My nails and my hair loosen,
The stiff flesh lurches and flows off like blood.

Grateful the surf of death drawing back under
(Offshore to fan out, vague and dark again)
My legs, my decayed feet, cock and heart.
If I were rid of them, somehow propped up . .
My vivid brain alone with a little vermilion!

The Pacifist's Song

I am the same yes as you others, only—
(Also for mé the plain where I was born,
Bore Her look, bear love, makes its mindless pull
And matters in my throat, also for me
The many-murdered sway my dreams unshorn,
Bearded with woe, their eyes blasted and dull)

Only I wake out of the vision of death
And hear One whisper whether man or god
"Kill not . . Your ill from evil comes . . Bear all";—
Only I must forsake my country's wrath
Who am earth's citizen, must human blood
Anywhere shed mourn, turning from it pale

Back to the old and serious labour, to
My restless labour under the vigilant stars,
From whom no broad storm ever long me hides.
What I try, doomed, is hard enough to do.
We breed up in our own breast our worse wars
Who long since sealed ourselves Hers Who abides.

Surviving Love

The clapper hovers, but why run so hard?
What he wants, has,—more than will make him ease;
No god calls down,—he's not been on his knees
This man, for years, and he is off his guard.
What then does he dream of
Sweating through day?—Surviving love.

Cold he knows he comes, once to the dark,
All that waste of cold, leaving all cold
Behind him hearts, forgotten when he's tolled,
His books are split and sold, the pencil mark
He made erased, his wife
Gone brave & quick to her new life.

And so he spins to find out something warm
To think on when the glaze fastens his eyes
And he begins to freeze. He slows and tries
To hear a promise: 'After, after your storm
I will grieve and remember,
Miss you and be warm and remember.'

But really nothing replies to the poor man,
He never hears this, or the voice he hears
(He thinks) he loses ah when next appears
The hood of the bell, seeing which he began.
His skull rings with his end,
He runs on, love for love.

The Lightning

Sick with the lightning lay my sister-in-law,
Concealing it from her children, when I came.
What I could, did, helpless with what I saw.

Analysands all, and the rest ought to be,
The friends my innocence cherished, and you and I,
Darling,—the friends I qualm and cherish and see.

. . The fattest nation!—wé do not thrive fat
But facile in the scale with all we rise
And shift a breakfast, and there is shame in that.

And labour sweats with vice at the top, and two
Bullies are bristling. What he thought who thinks?
It is difficult to say what one will do.

Obstinate, gleams from the black world the gay and fair,
My love loves chocolate, she loves also me,
And the lightning dances, but I cannot despair.

V

Rock-Study with Wanderer

'Cold cold cold of a special night'
Summer and winter sings under the beast
The ravished doll   Hear in the middle waste
The blue doll of the west cracking with fright

The music & the lights did not go out
Alas   Our foreign officers are gay
Singers in the faery cities shiver & play
Their exile dances through unrationed thought

Waiting for the beginning of the end
The wedding of the arms   Whose charnel arms
Will plough the emerald mathematical farms
In spring, spring-flowers to the U.N. send?

❀   ❀   ❀

Waiting I stroll within a summer wood
Avoiding broken glass in the slant sun
Our promises we may at last make good
The stained glass shies when the cathedral's won

Certainly in a few years call it peace
The arms & wings of peace patrol us all
The planes & arms that planes & arms may cease
Pathos (theanthropos) fills evenfall

When shall the body of the State come near
The body's state stable & labile? When

Irriding & resisting rage & fear
Shall men in unison yet resemble men?

Detroit our heart   When terribly we move
The sea is ours   We walk upon the sea
The air is ours   Hegemony, my love,
The good life's founded upon LST

The twilight birds wake   A paralysis
Is busy with societies and souls
Whose gnarled & pain-wild bodies beg abyss
Paraplegia dolorosa   The world rolls

A tired and old man resting on the grass
His forehead loose as if he had put away
Among the sun & the green & the young who pass
The whole long fever of his passionate day

. . To the dark watcher then an hour comes
Neither past nor future, when the chuffing sea
Far off like the rough of beast nearby succumbs
And a kind of sleep spreads over rock & tree

Nightshade not far from the abandoned tomb
Hangs its still bells & fatal berries down
The flowers dream   Crags shadows loom
The caresses of the animals are done

Under faint moon they lie absorbed and fair
Stricken their limbs flow in false attitudes
Of love   Dovetailed into a broken mirror
Stained famous glass are, where the watcher broods

All wars are civil   So the thing will die
Your civilization a glitter of great glass
The lusts have shivered you are shaken by
And step aside from in the moonlit grass

Stare on, cold riot of the western mind
Rockwalking man, what can a wanderer know?
Rattle departing of his friend and kind
And then (the widow sang) sphincter let go

         ❋   ❋   ❋

Draw draw the curtain on a little life
A filth a fairing   Wood is darkening
Where birdcall hovered now I hear no thing
I hours since came from my love my wife

Although a strange voice sometimes patiently
Near in the air when I lie vague and weak
As if it had a body tries to speak . . .
I must go back, she will be missing me

Whether There Is Sorrow in the Demons

Near the top a bad turn some dare. Well,
The horse swerves and screams, his eyes pop,
Feet feel air, the firm winds prop
Jaws wide wider until
Through great teeth rider greets the smiles of Hell.

Thick night, where the host's thews crack like thongs
A welcome, curving abrupt on cheek & neck.
No wing swings over once to check
Lick of their fire's tongues,
Whip & chuckle, hoarse insulting songs.

Powers immortal, fixed, intractable.
Only the lost soul jerks whom they joy hang:
Clap of remorse, and tang and fang
More frightful than the drill
An outsize dentist scatters down a skull;

Nostalgia rips him swinging. Fast in malice
How may his masters mourn, how ever yearn
The frore pride wherein they burn?
God's fire. To what *qui tollis*
Stone-tufted ears prick back towards the bright Palace?

Whence Lucifer shone Lucifer's friends hail
The scourge of choice made at the point of light
Destined into eternal night;
Motionless to fulfil
Their least, their envy looks up dense and pale.

. . Repine blackmarket felons; murderers
Sit still their time, till yellow feet go first,
Dies soon in them, and can die, thirst;
Not lives in these, nor years
On years scar their despair—which yet rehearse . . .

Their belvedere is black. They believe, and quail.
One shudder racks them only, lonely, and
No mirror breaks at their command.
Unsocketed, their will
Grinds on their fate. So was, so shall be still.

The Long Home

bulks where the barley blew, time out of mind
Of the sleepless Master. The barbered lawn
Far to a grey wall lounges, the birds are still,
Rising wind rucks from the sill
The slack brocade beside   the old throne he dreams on.
The portraits' hands are blind.

Below these frames they strain on stones. He mumbles . .
Fathers who listen, what loves hear
Surfacing from the lightless past? He foams.
Stillness locks a hundred rooms.
Louts in a bar aloud, The People, sucking beer.
A barefoot kiss. Who trembles?

Peach-bloom, sorb-apple sucked in what fine year!
I am a wine, he wonders; when?
Am I what I can do? My large white hands.
Boater & ascot, in grandstands
Coups. Concentrations of frightful cold, and then
Warm limbs below a pier.

The Master is sipping his identity.
Ardours & stars! Trash humped on trash.
The incorporated yacht, the campaign cheque
Signed one fall on the foredeck
Hard on a quarrel, to   amaze the fool. Who brash
Hectored out some false plea?

Brownpaper-blind, his morning passions trailed
Home in the clumsy dusk,—how now
Care which from which, trapped on a racing star

Where we know not who we are! . .
The whipcord frenzy curls, he slouches where his brow
Works like the rivals' failed.

Of six young men he flew to breakfast as,
Only the magpie, rapist, stayed
For dinner, and the rapist died, so that
Not the magpie but the cat
Vigil upon the magpie stalks, sulky parade,
Great tail switching like jazz.

Frightened, dying to fly, pied and obscene,
He blinks his own fantastic watch
For the indolent Spring of what he was before;
A stipple of sunlight, clouded o'er,
Remorse a scribble on   the magic tablet which
A schoolboy thumb jerks clean.

Heat lightning straddles the horizon dusk
Above the yews: the fresh wind blows:
He flicks a station on by the throne-side . .
Out in the wide world, Kitty—wide
Night—*far across the sea* . . . Some guardian accent
    grows
Below the soft voice, brusque:

"You are: not what you wished but what you were,
The decades' vise your gavel brands,
You glare the god who gobbled his own fruit,
He who stood mute, lucid and mute,
Under peine forte et dure to will his bloody lands,
Then whirled down without heir."

The end of which he will not know. Undried,
A prune-skin helpless on his roof.
His skin gleams in the lamplight dull as gold
And old gold clusters like mould
Stifling about his blood, time's helm to build him proof.
Thump the oak, and preside!

An ingrown terrible smile unflowers, a sigh
Blurs, the axle turns, unmanned.
Habited now forever with his weight
Well-housed, he rolls in the twilight
Unrecognizable   against the world's rim, and
A bird whistles nearby.

Whisked off, a voice, fainter, faint, a guise,
A gleam, pin of a, a. Nothing.
—One look round last, like rats, before we leave.
A famous house. Now the men arrive:
Horror, they swing their cold   bright mallets, they're
        breaking
Him up before my eyes!

Wicked vistas! The wolves mourn for our crime
Out past the grey wall. On to our home,
Whereby the barley may seed and resume.
Mutter of thrust stones palls this room,
The crash of mallets. He   is going where I come.
Barefoot soul fringed with rime.

A Winter-Piece to a Friend Away

Your letter came.—Glutted the earth & cold
With rains long heavy, follows intense frost;
      Snow howls and hides the world
We workt awhile to build; all the roads are lost;
Icy spiculae float, filling strange air;
No voice goes far; one is alone whirling since where,
      And when was it one crossed?
      You have been there.

I too the breaking blizzard's eddies bore
One year, another year: tempted to drop
      At my own feet forlorn
Under the warm fall, frantic more to chop
Wide with the gale until my thought ran numb
Clenching the blue skin tight against what white spikes
         come,
      And the sick brain estop.
      Your pendulum
Mine, not stilled wholly, has been sorry for,
Weeps from, and would instruct . . Unless I lied
      What word steadies that cord?
Glade grove & ghyll of antique childhood glide
Off; from our grown grief, weathers that appal,
The massive sorrow of the mental hospital,
      Friends & our good friends hide.
      They came to call.

Hardly theirs, moment when the tempest gains,
Loose heart convulses. Their hearts bend off dry,
      Their fruit dangles and fades.

—Solicitudes of the orchard heart, comply
A little with my longing, a little sing
Our sorrow among steel & glass, our stiffening,
    That hers may modify:
    O trembling Spring.—

Immortal risks our sort run, to a house
Reported in a wood . . . mould upon bread
    And brain, breath giving out,
From farms we go by, barking, and shaken head,
The shrunk pears hang, Hölderlin's weathercock
Rattles to tireless wind, the fireless landscape rock,
    Artists insane and dead
    Strike like a clock:

If the fruit is dead, fast. Wait. Chafe your left wrist.
All these too lie, whither a true form strays.
    Sweet when the lost arrive.
Foul sleet ices the twigs, the vision frays,
Festoons all signs; still as I come to name
My joy to you my joy springs up again the same,—
    The thaw alone delays,—
    Your letter came!

New Year's Eve

The grey girl who had not been singing stopped,
And a brave new no-sound blew through acrid air.
I set my drink down, hard. Somebody slapped
Somebody's second wife somewhere,
Wheeling away to long to be alone.
I see the dragon of years is almost done,
Its claws loosen, its eyes
Crust now with tears & lust and a scale of lies.

A whisky-listless and excessive saint
Was expounding his position, whom I hung
Boy-glad in glowing heaven: he grows faint:
Hearing what song the sirens sung,
Sidelong he web-slid and some rich prose spun.
The tissue golden of the gifts undone
Surpassed the gifts. Miss Weirs
Whispers to me her international fears.

Intelligentsia milling. In a semi-German
(Our loss of Latin fractured how far our fate,—
Disinterested once, linkage once like a sermon)
I struggle to articulate
Why it is our promise breaks in pieces early.
The Muses' visitants come soon, go surly
With liquor & mirrors away
In this land wealthy & casual as a holiday.

Whom the Bitch winks at. Most of us are linsey-
woolsey workmen, grandiose, and slack.
On m'analyse, the key to secrets. Kinsey
Shortly will tell us sharply back

Habits we stuttered. How revive to join
(Great evils grieve beneath: eye Caesar's coin)
And lure a while more home
The vivid wanderers, uneasy with our shame?

Priests of the infinite! ah, not for long.
The dove whispers, and diminishes
Up the blue leagues. And no doubt we heard wrong—
Wax of our lives collects & dulls; but was
What we heard hurried as we memorized,
Or brightened, or adjusted? Undisguised
We pray our tongues & fingers
Record the strange word that blows suddenly and
    lingers.

Imagine a patience in the works of love
Luck sometimes visits. Ages we have sighed,
And cleave more sternly to a music of
Even this sore word 'genocide'.
Each to his own! Clockless & thankless dream
And labour Makers, being what we seem.
Soon soon enough we turn
Our tools in; brownshirt Time chiefly our works will
    burn.

I remember: white fine flour everywhere whirled
Ceaselessly, wheels rolled, a slow thunder boomed,
And there were snowy men in the mill-world
With sparkling eyes, light hair uncombed,
And one of them was humming an old song,
Sack upon sack grew portly, until strong
Arms moved them on, by pairs,
And then the bell clanged and they ran like hares.

Scotch in his oxter, my Retarded One
Blows in before the midnight; freezing slush
Stamps off, off. Worst of years! . . no matter, begone;
Your slash and spells (in the sudden hush)
We see now we had to suffer some day, so
I cross the dragon with a blessing, low,
While the black blood slows. Clock-wise,
We clasp upon the stroke, kissing with happy cries.

OF *1947*

Narcissus Moving

Noise of the vans woke us before we would
At the second landing a fine mirror cracked
Scratches appeared on all the valued wood
And this was the Fairway's last official act

Unfit to form attachment he is flying
The weather favours jokers of this kind
News of the hairy cousins was supplying
Barkers with gossip not to speak his mind

Blond to the dawn comes down himself in green
Verging on joy   I see his knuckles white
With joy and yet he stood all night unseen
In reverie upstairs under the skylight

The neglected corners said what they were for
'Limpid the lapse & sweet relapse of water
Upon my trembling image, ah, no more'
He whispered and stole downstairs to the slaughter

With a bannister he laid a blue bone bare
A tongue tore hard but one boot in a groin
Sank like a drift   A double fist of hair
Like feathers members that will not rejoin

Flat slams below there but I blew my drag
Against my ash and strained, ash on the tile
Spoilt the good washroom, weary with a jag
I chinned the sill to watch a wicked mile

The walls of stone bury to some pavanne
The garden   A bloody rubbish a dancing shoe
'Two-Eyes could bear no more' like the dusty swan
Shut of its cage and doubtful what to do

A vile tune from the shattered radio
Incredibly arises & dies at once . . .
A deeper silence, then we slowly know
Somewhere in the empty mansion one tap runs

'A Negress gnawed my lip up a terrible place
Why not? the rising sun will light me poor'
Only upon a young man's most blond face
Une silence de la mort de l'amour

The Dispossessed

'and something that . . that is theirs—no longer ours'
stammered to me the Italian page. A wood
seeded & towered suddenly. I understood.—

The Leading Man's especially, and the Juvenile Lead's,
and the Leading Lady's thigh that switches & warms,
and their grimaces, and their flying arms:

our arms, our story. Every seat was sold.
A crone met in a clearing sprouts a beard
and has a tirade. Not a word we heard.

Movement of stone within a woman's heart,
abrupt & dominant. They gesture how
fings really are. Rarely a child sings now.

My harpsichord weird as a koto drums
adagio for twilight, for the storm-worn dove
no more de-iced, and the spidery business of love.

The Juvenile Lead's the Leader's arm, one arm
running the whole bole, branches, roots, (O watch)
and the faceless fellow waving from her crotch,

Stalin-unanimous! who procured a vote
and care not use it, who have kept an eye
and care not use it, percussive vote, clear eye.

That which a captain and a weaponeer
one day and one more day did, we did, *ach*
we did not, *They* did . . cam slid, the great lock

lodged, and no soul of us all was near was near,—
an evil sky (where the umbrella bloomed)
twirled its mustaches, hissed, the ingenue fumed,

poor virgin, and no hero rides. The race
is done. Drifts through, between the cold black trunks,
the peachblow glory of the perishing sun

in empty houses where old things take place.

HIS THOUGHT MADE POCKETS
& THE PLANE BUCKT

TO ANN

Henry sats in de plane & was gay.
Careful Henry nothing said aloud
but where a virgin out of cloud
to her Mountain dropt in light
his thought made pockets & the plane buckt.
"Parm me, Lady." "Orright."

Venice, 182-

White & blue my breathing lady leans
across me in the first light, so we kiss.
The corners of her eyes are white. I miss,
renew. She means
to smother me thro' years of this.

Hell chill young widows in the heel of night—
perduring loves, melody's thrusting, press
flush with the soft skin, whence they sprung! back. Less
ecstasy might
save us for speech & politeness.

I hear her howl now, and I slam my eyes
against the glowing face. Foul morning-cheese
stands fair compared to love. On waspish knees
our pasts surprise
and plead us livid. Now she frees

a heavy lock was pulling . . . I kiss it,
lifting my hopeless lids—and all trace
of passion's vanisht from her eyes & face,
the lip I bit
is bluer, a blackhead at the base

of her smooth nose looks sullenly at me,
we look at each other in entire despair,
her eyes are swimming by mine, and I swear
sobbing quickly
we àre in love. The light hurts. "There . . ."

Scots Poem

Loversgrove lay
off to the lighthearted south,
chat-south, miles & more miles. Weel,
mot-tive flunks a man's mouth seems full of teeth.

Peered at her long
sidewise and would not or could
not say Love will be leaping
hopeless forever, hard on one who stood

near to her long
till she lookt poorly and died.
Braird in the breast evergreen,
grey the fieldgrass though, man's friend. I'm inside.—

—Trumpet shall sound,
angel & archangel cry
"Come forth, Isobel Mitchel,
and meet William Matheson in the sky."

Sonnet XXV

Sometimes the night echoes to prideless wailing
low as I hunch home late & fever-tired
near you not, nearing the sharer I desired
toward whom till now I sailed back, but that sailing
yaws, from the cabin orders like a failing
dribble, the stores disordered & then fired
skid wild, the men are glaring, the mate has wired
"Hopeless." Lockt in & humming, the Captain's nailing
a false log to the lurching table. Lies
& passion sing in the cabin on the voyage home,
the burgee should fly Jolly Roger. Wind
madness like the tackle of a crane—outcries
ascend—around to heave him from the foam
irresponsible, since all the stars rain blind.

The Mysteries
(A CRAZED MAN CALLS)

And now you be my guest.
Thinking like wings, solemn with moons & truth,
I accost you on a summit of your honour
Erich Kahler for you shoot like a tooth
where you grill, if others glare in wonder,
you too have to come out

and now you be my guest.
At the trice of harvest to a middle ground
I ascend and seek the hollow of my tree
central in a grove and call: cherry sound
swelling through swart night, near the sea, near sea,
men aye did charm abroad

And now you be my guest
for peace to peace will not assuage or answer
my goddess at the Cross-ways. Crown the gong!
Rears the first fox, and ducks, and is a dancer!
The stonechat clatters in the bracken! Song
through flutes shrugs up from bronze

and now you be my guest.
In the sea-green blindness I found Thetis kind
and you will find me with you. I must sing
passions unended while you are turning, blind,
great blows thukk in darkness, thickening
cymbals, a small hand waves,

and so you be my guest
uncircling, you who were a dancing man

dance in darkness! Drips off our grapes blood,
they scream, the child is swinging on the fan,
a purpose tightens in the thigh of god
like your heart in the drums' thunder

and now you be my guest
while leaping mouths rage forward and white eyes,
coarse night between smooth laurel boles, crowns shove
and crack to be timely at the sacrifice
where I go to pieces. I am lived by love,
and I am partly dying

and now you be my guest
so we go, one, for wineless ecstasy
and whether will ever either back O turn
is known, and the snow is hovering over the sea
and the child cries, and worshippers will burn
the sweet lost leaves of my trees.

They Have

A thing O say a sixteenth of an inch
long, with whiskers
& wings it doesn't use, & many legs,
has all this while been wandering in a tiny space
on the black wood table by my burning chair.
I see it has a feeler of some length
it puts out before it.
That must be how it was following the circuit
of the bottom of my wine-glass, vertical: Mâcon: I thought
it smelt & wanted some but couldn't get hold.
Now here's another thing, on my paper, a fluff
of legs, and I blow: my brothers & sisters go away.
But here he's back, & got between the pad
& padback, where I save him and
shift him to my blue shirt, where he is.
The other little one's gone somewhere else.
They have things easy.

The Poet's Final Instructions

Dog-tired, suisired, will now my body down
near Cedar Avenue in Minneap,
when my crime comes. I am blazing with hope.
Do me glory, come the whole way across town.

I couldn't rest from hell just anywhere,
in commonplaces. Choiring & strange my pall!
I might not lie still in the waste of St Paul
or buy DAD's root beer; good signs I forgive.

Drop here, with honour due, my trunk & brain
among the passioning of my countrymen
unable to read, rich, proud of their tags
and proud of me. Assemble all my bags!
Bury me in a hole, and give a cheer,
near Cedar on Lake Street, where the used cars live.

from *The Black Book* (*i*)

Grandfather, sleepless in a room upstairs,
seldom came down; so when they tript him down
we wept. The blind light sang about his ears,
later we heard. Brother had pull. In pairs
he, some, slept upon stone.
Later they stamped him down in mud.
The windlass drew him silly & odd-eyed, blood
broke from his ears before they quit.
Before they trucked him home they cleaned him up somewhat.

Only the loose eyes' glaze they could not clean
and soon he died. He howled a night and shook
our teeth before the end; we breathed again
when he stopt. Abraham, what we have seen
write, I beg, in your Book.
No more the solemn and high bells
call to our pall; we call or gibber; Hell's
irritable & treacherous
despairs here here (not him) reach now to shatter us.

from *The Black Book* (*ii*)

Luftmenschen dream, the men who live on air,
of other values, in the blackness watching
peaceful for gangs or a quick raid,
the ghetto nods a mortal head
soundless but for a scurry, a sigh, retching,—
no moan of generation fear.
Hands hold each other limper
while the moon lengthens on the sliding river.

Prolong the woolen night—Solomon sang—
and never the soul with its own revenge encumber
but like a cry of cranes dies out,
ecstatic, faint, a moment float-
ing, flying soul, or flares like August timber
in wild woe vanishing.
Blue grows from grey, towards slaughter.
(An Ashkenazi genius stoned Ivan; a sculptor.)

"Boleslaus brought us here, surnamed the Good,
whose dust rolls nearly seven hundred years
towards Sirius; we thank that King
as for the ledge whereto we cling,
night in the caves under the ruins; stars,
armbands come off, for which we could
be glad but the black troops gather."
So those who kneel in the paling sky & shiver.

Dawn like a rose unfolds—flower of parks—
alleys of limetrees, villas, ponds, a palace
down a deserted riverbed,
the Lazienki Gardens' pride,

monument to a king able and callous
who far Vienna from the Turks
bloodily did deliver.
For foreigners, now, a sort of theatre.

One officer in black demarches here
cupshot, torn collar by a girl unwilling
native & blond through the debauch
that kept him all night from his couch,
hurts his head and from the others' howling
drove him out for morning air.
Brooding over the water
he reddens suddenly. He went back & shot her.

from *The Black Book* (*iii*)

Lover & child, a little sing.
From long-lockt cattle-cars who grope
who near a place of showers come
foul no more, whose murmuring
grows in a hiss of gas will clear them home:
Away from & toward me: a little soap,
disrobing, *Achtung!* in a dirty hope,
they shuffle with their haircuts in to die.
Lift them an elegy, poor you and I,
fair & strengthless as seafoam
under a deserted sky.

A Sympathy, A Welcome

Feel for your bad fall how could I fail,
poor Paul, who had it so good.
I can offer you only: this world like a knife.
Yet you'll get to know your mother
and humourless as you do look you will laugh
and all the others
will NOT be fierce to you, and loverhood
will swing your soul like a broken bell
deep in a forsaken wood, poor Paul,
whose wild bad father loves you well.

Not to Live
(JAMESTOWN 1957)

It kissed us, soft, to cut our throats, this coast,
like a malice of the lazy King. I hunt,
& hunt! but find here what to kill?—nothing is blunt,
but phantoming uneases I find. Ghost
on ghost precedes of all most scared us, most
we fled. Howls fail upon this secret, far air: grunt,
shaming for food; you must. I love the King
& it was not I who strangled at the toast
but a flux of a free & dying adjutant:
God be with him. He & God be with us all,
for we are not to live. I cannot wring,
like laundry, blue my soul—indecisive thing. . . .
From undergrowth & over odd birds call
and who would starv'd so survive? God save the King.

American Lights, Seen from Off Abroad

Blue go up & blue go down
to light the lights of Dollartown

Nebuchadnezzar had it so good?
wink the lights of Hollywood

I never think, I have so many things,
flash the lights of Palm Springs

I worry like a madwoman over all the world,
affirm the lights, all night, at State

I have no plans, I mean well,
swear the lights of Georgetown

I have the blind staggers
call the lights of Niagara

We shall die in a palace
shout the black lights of Dallas

I couldn't dare less, my favorite son,
fritter the lights of Washington

(I have a brave old So-and-So,
chuckle the lights of Independence, Mo.)

I cast a shadow, what I mean,
blurt the lights of Abilene

Both his sides are all the same
glows his grin with all but shame

He can do nothing night & day'
wonder his lovers. So they say.

"Basketball in outer space"
sneers the White New Hampshire House

I'll have a smaller one, later, Mac,
hope the strange lights of Cal Tech

I love you one & all, hate shock,
bleat the lights of Little Rock

I cannot quite focus
cry the lights of Las Vegas

I am a maid of shots & pills,
swivel the lights of Beverly Hills

Proud & odd, you give me vertigo,
fly the lights of San Francisco

I am all satisfied love & chalk,
mutter the great lights of New York

I have lost your way
say the white lights of Boston

Here comes a scandal to blight you to bed.
Here comes a cropper.' That's what I said.

(Lévanto, 7 october 1957)

Note to Wang Wei

How could you be so happy, now some thousand years
disheveled, puffs of dust?
It leaves me uneasy at last,
your poems teaze me to the verge of tears
and your fate. It makes me think.
It makes me long for mountains & blue waters.
Makes me wonder how much to allow.
(I'm reconfirming, God of bolts & bangs,
of fugues & bucks, whose rocket burns & sings.)
I wish we could meet for a drink
in a "freedom from ten thousand matters."
Be dust myself pretty soon; not now.

FORMAL ELEGY

Formal Elegy

I

A hurdle of water, and O these waters are cold
(warm at outset) in the dirty end.
Murder on murder on murder, where I stagger,
whiten the good land where we have held out.
These kills were not for loot,
however Byzantium hovers in the mind:
were matters of principle—that's worst of all—
& fear & crazed mercy.
Ruby, with his mad claim
he shot to spare the Lady's testifying,
probably is sincere.
No doubt, in his still cell, his mind sits pure.

II

Yes, it looks like a wilderness—pacem appellant.
Honour to Patrolman Tippit. Peace to the rifler's widow.
Seven, I believe, play fatherless.

III

Scuppered the yachts, the choppers, big cars, jets.
Nobody goes anywhere,
lengthened (days) into TV.
I am four feet long, invisibly.
What in the end will be left of us is a stare,
underwater.
If you want me to join you in confident prayer, let's
not.
I sidled in & past, gazing upon it,
the bier.

IV

Too Andean hopes, now angry shade.—
I am an automobile. Into me climb
many, and go their ways. Onto him climbed
a-many and went his way.
For a while we seemed to be having a holiday
off from ourselves—ah, but the world is wigs,
as sudden we came to feel
and even his splendid hair kept not wholly real
fumbling & falsing in & out of the Bay of Pigs,
the bad moment of this excellent man,
suffered by me as a small car can.
Faithful to course we stayed.

V

Some in their places are constrained to weep.
Stunned, more, though.
Black foam. A weaving snake. An invulnerable sleep.
It doing have to come so.
All at once, hurtless, in the tide of applause
& expectation. I write from New York
where except for a paraplegic exterminator—
a gracious & sweet guy—
nobody has done no work
lately

VI

It's odd perhaps that Dallas   cannot after their crimes
criminals protect or Presidents.
Fat Dallas, a fit set.
I would not perhaps have voted for him next time.
Images of Mr Kennedy blue the air,

who is little now, with no chance to grow great,
but who have set his touch across the State,
true-intended, strong

VII
My breath comes heavy, does my breath.
I feel heavy about the President's death.

VIII
I understand I hear I see I read
schoolgirls in Dallas when the white word came
or slammed, cheered in their thoughtful grades,
brought-up to a loving tone.
I do not sicken but somewhat with shame
I shift my head an inch; who are my own.
I have known a loving Texas   woman in parades
and she was boastful & treacherous.
That boringest of words, whereas here I blush,
"education," peters to a nailing of us.

IX
An editor has asked me in my name
what wish or prophecy I'd like to state
for the new year. I am silent on these occasions
steadily, having no love for a fool
(which I keep being) but I break my rule:
I do all-wish the bullets swim astray
sent to the President, and that all around
help, and his heart keep sound.
I have a strange sense

                he's about to be the best of men.
Amen.

X

It's quiet at Arlington. Rock Creek is quiet.
My prīmers, with Mount Auburn. Everybody should
have his sweet boneyards. Yet let the young not go,
our apprentice King! Alas,
muffled, he must. He seemed good:
brainy in riot, daring, cool.

                              So
let us abandon the scene of disorder. Drop
them shattered bodies into tranquil places,
where moulder as you will. We compose our faces
cold as the cresting waters; ready again.
The waters break.
All black & white together, stunned, survive
the final insolence to the head of you;
bow.
Overwhelmed-un, live.
A rifle fact is over, pistol facts
almost entirely are too.
The man of a wise face opened it to speak:
Let us continue.

71
72
74
75
76
77
79
80
83
85